# Issa: Cup-of-Tea Poems

# Issa:
# Cup-of-Tea Poems

## Selected Haiku of Kobayashi Issa

Translated from Japanese by
David G. Lanoue

ASIAN HUMANITIES PRESS
Berkeley, California

ASIAN HUMANITIES PRESS/AHP Paperbacks

Asian Humanities Press offers to the specialist and the general reader alike, the best in new translations of major works and significant original contributions, to enhance our understanding of Asian literature, religions, cultures and thought. "Asian Humanities Press" and "AHP Paperbacks" are trademarks of Jain Publishing Company.

**Library of Congress Cataloging-in-Publication Data**

Kobayashi, Issa, 1763-1827.
    [Poems. English. Selections]
    Issa, Cup-of-tea poems: selected haiku of Kobayashi Issa / translated from Japanese by David G. Lanoue.
       p.   cm.
    Translation of: Issa zenshū, v. 1: Shinano Mainichi Shinbunsha. 1979.
    ISBN 0-89581-874-4
    1. Kobayashi, Issa, 1763-1827—Translations, English.
2. Haiku—translations into English. 3. Haiku, English—Translations from Japanese. I. Lanoue, David G. II. Title.
PL797.2.A25   1991
895.6'13—dc20                    91-4376
                                                  CIP

*for Bryan*

# *Acknowledgements*

I thank my mentor, Paul A. Olson of the University of Nebraska; Robert Spiess, editor of *Modern Haiku*; and my colleagues at the 1989 N. E. H. Literary Translation Institute—who have all helped me with their criticism, suggestions, and encouragement. Thanks also to Hugh Kenner, for kind commentary; to Takako Kawano, who taught me Japanese; to Xavier University of Louisiana that has supported me; and to my students, who have always been a boundless, generous source of insight. Finally, I thank Mr. Takashi Kubota, who kindly hosted me for two summers of study in Japan and who, only days after our first meeting, drove me personally from Tokyo to Issa's home village in the mountains, just because he knew it would help.

Some of the translations in this book first appeared in *Modern Haiku*, Summer and Fall, 1990.

## TEXTUAL NOTE

The translations in this book are based on original texts found in *Issa Zenshū*, Vol. I, Shinano Mainichi Shimbunsha, 1979.

# *Illustrations*

All of the illustrations are photo-reproduced enlargements of Issa's original calligraphy taken from the original manuscripts of various poetic diaries and haiku anthologies.

しなのおと　庭首欣一筆書

# Cup-of-Tea Poet

Kobayashi Issa (1763-1827) is at once the most profoundly devout and down-in-the-mud silly of all the great masters of Japanese haiku. A Buddhist priest of the Jōdoshinshū sect, Issa approaches the natural miracles of this world evenly, showing the same reverent awe and artistic excitement for plum trees in full bloom and dog crap covered by a light snow. Though his society was one still clinging to stiff feudal hierarchy, where lords, samurai, priests, merchants, farmers, prostitutes, beggars—all knew their roles by heart—Issa's poetic vision is liberating, iconoclastic, democratic. He presents whatever is, here and now, refusing to screen out experiences that do not conform to the "party-line"—political or poetic.

Because he was perceived in his own time and by posterity as an outsider, a rebel and a voice for common folk; Issa has enjoyed a growing, broad-based popularity in his native Japan. Japanese critics have enshrined him (along with Bashō, Buson and Shiki) as one of the top four masters of haiku, and it is nearly impossible to meet a Japanese person today who has not memorized, in elementary school, two or three of Issa's most famous poems. As with his English contemporary William Blake, many of Issa's poems became staples of children's literature in his country after his death. However, also like Blake, Issa's genius has been as widely acknowledged by his adult readers. In his most ingenuous, "child's eye" poems, one finds an absolute control of language, a brilliantly conceived Buddhist vision of a living, dynamic cosmos, and, at times, political protest. A famous example of all this is a haiku that most Japanese schoolchildren know by heart:

> scrawny
> frog
> fight
> on!
> Issa
> to
> the
> rescue

Children delight in the wonderful comedy of a grown man crouched down to a frog level, vowing to rescue a skinny frog locked in a mock-epic (losing) battle over croaking rights in a pond. Many of their adult counterparts have praised Issa's willingness to defend the downtrodden, if only in the imaginary act of poetry. Born in the small farming village of Kashiwabara, in a poor mountainous province then-called Shinano, Issa styled himself, "Shinano Province's Head Beggar," and was famous for his eccentric, poor-artist's lifestyle in the tumble-down house he called, affectionately, his *kuzu-ya*, "trash-house." On a political level Issa's skinny frog haiku suggests a poetic overthrow of the "might makes right" mentality of Edo period emperor/daimyo/samurai-controlled Japan, in which "big frogs" inevitably came out on top. And, if one reflects on the poem in light of Issa's Buddhist vision of reality (expressed in countless poetic and prose passages throughout his journals), his frog-defence could even reflect the saving power of the Amida Buddha (more on this later). Issa imbues even his most childlike verses with a mature Buddhist faith to profound poetic effect.

It is little wonder, then, that in translation Issa has become an international treasure. Every year more widely published, translated and admired in East and West, he speaks plainly across cultures of a simple life based on gentle respect and genuine love for this living, fragile planet. Readers need not delve into the arcana of Japanese Buddhism to decode the haiku of "Priest-Issa." Their spirituality, wisdom and down-to-earth humor translate naturally into Western languages. Furthermore, Issa's ecological poetry approaches nature respectfully, with unclouded expectant eyes, and is possibly more relevant today than it was in the first quarter of the 19th century. We have reached the point in our history as a species in which we are crying out for a poetry that will invite us home: to hear our birds, walk in our mist, notice our fleas, celebrate our blossoms.

I have mentioned that Issa's haiku are Buddhist in tone and purpose. The poet was a practising lay-priest of the Jōdoshinshū, or New Pure Land sect, and a little background knowledge of this most popular of Japanese sects is as essential for understanding Issa as an appreciation of Catholic theology is for making sense of Dante. Jōdoshinshū subscribes

to a universe that is dancing in constant creative
transformation as sentient beings, in life after life,
grow slowly toward enlightenment: "rebirth" in
Amida Buddha's Pure Land. For humans this rebirth
need not be something one must wait for after death,
but an immediate, living experience that Issa attempts
to recapture in every haiku he writes. Each of his
poems is an "awakening" to a universe in which
apparent divisions and differences resolve in the
boundless, saving reality of the Buddha. Thus, in
Issa's haiku beggars are rich, lords are poor; even
the boundary line drawn between human and animal
is happily bridged as fleas, frogs and flies share his
loneliness, boredom, sadness or ecstacy. Issa fondly
regards animals as fellow travelers on the pilgrimage
of existence. In a Buddhist universe that admits
reincarnation, it is not pathetic fallacy to find
"human" emotions in even a fly. The fly Issa swats
at is a cousin.

One of the secrets to Issa's universal appeal
across cultures is his skill in creating poetic surprises
in which the reader's expectations are suddenly,
delightfully derailed. His haiku cross the lines sepa-
rating emperor and peasant, poet and frog, the ideal
and the mundane, the beautiful and the scatological.
In Issa's poetry of surprise exquisite cherry blossoms
end up stuck in mud; a delicate first snow faintly
covers dog crap; lotuses (symbols of rebirth and
Buddhist salvation) sprout in sewer water; the long
autumn night is punctuated with farts; a dewy field is
irrigated by the poet taking a leak; cats mating behind
a hedge comically are described as courtly lovers

from the *Tale of Genji*.

Issa's ironic boundary-crossing poems perfectly express his Pure Land Buddhist way of being in, and viewing, the world. In Jōdoshinshū Buddhism the key to salvation—to rebirth in the Western Paradise —lies in simply, absolutely trusting in the Amida Buddha. This age (*mappō*) is a corrupt and fallen one in which it has become next to impossible for sinners to extricate themselves, by their own ego-tainted efforts, from attachments to the goods of the earth, and so it is difficult to attain the liberated, awakened Buddha-state. "Simply trust" is advice found throughout Issa's poems and journals. His Amidist trusting in "the Beyond" amounts to a happy indifference to whatever the future holds for him, whether it be the pit of deepest Hell or Buddha's Pure Land. His trusting, accepting indifference, born of faith, allows him to glimpse Paradise here and now, a transfigured reality in which lords and beggars, men and flies, snow and what a dog leaves in the road—joyously arise in the *dharmakāya*: the body of the One.

In writing this translation, I have adopted as a working premise that Issa's poetry and religion are one thing. He directs readers to come to this conclusion in many, many passages. For example:

new
spring
Yatarō
dies
priest
Issa
is
born

In this New Year's Day haiku (in the old lunar calendar the year's first day coincides with the beginning of spring), the poet triumphantly announces his rebirth. Dead is Yatarō, born is Issa, "Cup-of-Tea," priest. In a later version he ends this poem with the phrase: "born is Issa of the Temple of Haiku." Every line of his poetry, he suggests, is prayer.

More could be written (and has been, most of it in Japanese) on Issa's poetry in relation to the world-view and salvation scheme of Jōdoshinshū Buddhism, but for our purpose, one should at least be aware of the main tenets set down in the 13th century by the sect's founder, Shinran, and keep these in mind while reading Issa:

1. This age is a fallen one in which individuals, by their own power, are unable to realize enlightenment/awakening/Buddhahood. Selfishly we cling to illusions of "mine" and "yours"—tragically attempting to grasp the transitory goods of this earth even as they are slipping away, fading like dewdrops, like mist, like melting snow.

2. Salvation lies in the vow of Amida Buddha, who pledged to delay his own entry into nirvana

until all who call upon his name with sincere heart would be assured of salvation: rebirth in the Pure Land, the Western Paradise.

3. Not by striving, but by simply, utterly trusting in the Buddha and in his vow does one attain release from the Hell of attachments. The fallen ungraspable world is now transfigured, shining with life, light, Buddhahood. Viewed with enlightened eyes, *this* is the Pure Land; we are, and always have been, the one Buddha.

4. Praising Buddha with the chant, "Namu Amida Butsu," is not a request to be saved but rather a spontaneous, joyful outburst of gratitude for the miracle of salvation already factually brought about by the "Other Power" of the Buddha at work in our lives. (Note: I translate "Namu Amida Butsu" as "praising Buddha" when this phrase occurs in the haiku).

Issa's poetry is all about trusting in the elusive moments of this world: catching glimpses into a transformed reality brimming with love and meaning and beauty. Haiku, for priest Cup-of-Tea, is revelation.

Because of his abiding Pure Land Buddhist faith, Issa's haiku vision of the universe is at heart comic. This may surprise readers who associate the poet with dreary biographical details: the loss of his mother in childhood, a severe stepmother, the deaths of four children in infancy followed by that of his first wife, and his many poignant poems written about dewdrop worlds, loss, sorrow. Yet the overall tone of Issa's complete works—thousands of haiku written over the course of a lifetime dedicated to his art—is not tragic, if we define the tragic gesture as an attempt to grasp this fleeting world. If, conversely, we define the comic attitude as one of relinquishing one's attempts to grasp the flux—of stepping back from the game and declaring victory in laughter—then Issa's Jōdoshinshū Buddhist faith undergirds an emphatically comic poetry.

*        *        *

In Japanese, a haiku consists of seventeen "syllables" (*onji*) arranged in a 5-7-5 pattern short enough to be recited in one breath. A "seasonal word" is almost always present, linking the individual poem with the vast, archetypal pattern of the Year of Life.

A haiku does not label itself, apologize for itself, attempt to explain itself. It is untitled and stands alone, not needing windy explication to prop it up. A haiku just is. As a haiku is not so much an intellective or cognitive poem as it is one of awareness, felt-depth, perception through the senses, of insight and intuition by the heart, my first concern as a translator always has been to create in English the core feeling of each poem, following closely Issa's own vocabulary: unadorned, colloquial, yet arresting. Since many of his haiku are carefully ordered "surprises" or revelations, I also try to respect as closely as possible the original ordering of images. For example, Issa writes:

snow
melting
village
brimming
over
kids

and:

locked
in
a
staring
contest
with
a
frog

These haiku build up to poetic punch lines: "Snow melting village brimming over . . . kids!" and "Locked in a staring contest with . . . a frog!" It would be capricious and violate the revelatory structure of these poems to render them: "Children flood the village of melting snow" and "A frog is having a staring-match with me," but, sadly, many of Issa's English translators willfully tinker with his original ordering of images and in the process utterly "spoil the joke."

I have not divided the text according to the conventional seasonal headings of "Spring," "Summer," "Autumn," and "Winter." I want nothing to detract from the reader's focus on the poems themselves— on finding Issa in Issa, not in commentary, trivia or a clutter of labels. The haiku themselves, one read after another, comprise a musical journey through the seasons of life, from spring to winter, birth to death, with images and meanings accumulating over time as individual poems reflect one another, answer one another, harmonize with one another in one symphonic movement.

Readers who are familiar with haiku in English may be surprised at the vertical one-word-a-line structure that I have chosen here. The more I read Japanese haiku, the more I am convinced that it is an art of step-by-step accumulation, as word builds on word into a single, resonant compound. To take an example from Issa's great predecessor, Bashō:

> old
> pond
> a
> frog
> jumps
> in
> water
> sound

Presented vertically, the haiku forces the reader to dwell, ever-so-briefly, on each word, each building step in the sequence toward full revelation. In my opinion, there is more of the freshness of the original in this arrangement than one finds in the usual three-line English format.

I close this introduction with a final comment on how to read haiku, after which I will allow Issa to speak for himself. Issa, like all true masters of the form, invites the reader to partake not of abstract ideas but of experience—palpable, wondrous encounters with life: a swallow bursting out the nose of a great bronze Buddha, cows moo-mooing in thick autumn mist, a butterfly resting on a dog curled to sleep. Even his brushwork in the manuscripts (as seen in the illustrations) suggests a spontaneous, scribbling-down-the-page-fast-and-furious response to the elusive present moment. Therefore, one does not read such poetry in a greedy rush to understand a theme, a point or a concept. Rather, we do best by Issa if we open ourselves to each haiku with the same non-grasping attention we might pay to a bird warbling in a tree. After all, the poet himself insists that birdsong is haiku:

> like
> warbling
> pure
> haiku
> mountain
> cuckoo

Like a bird twittering one-breath improvisations deep in the summer cedars on some shady fathomless Japanese mountainside, Issa creates vivid, non-intellectual expressions of life on a living planet. The haiku moment awaits the reader who patiently allows words on the page to register as deeply felt reality.

Issa: Cup-of-Tea Poems

月お夜さもちゝ位ゑおゝ春

new
spring
Yatarō
dies
priest
Issa
is
born

a
bright
kite
soars
a
beggar's
shack
below


my
ecstacy
about
average
my
spring

the
year's
first
rain
a
grass
roof's
first
leak


tumble-down
house
no
different
spring
begins

in
the
Buddha
trusting
spring
begins

*Issa: Cup-of-Tea Poems*

New
Year's
Day
no
different
trashy
house

made
with
sooty
paper
the
stepchild's
kite


snow
melting
village
brimming
over
kids

snow
melting
the
beggar-town's
thin
children


pee-hole
pocked
leftover
melting
snow

on
Buddha's
temple
clinging
leftover
snow

misty
day
windows
solid
blank
prison

precious
harp
beggar's
flute
deep
in
mist

vespers
bell
in
mist
life
slipping
by

misty
day
even
Heaven's
saints
bored
stiff

rap-a-tap
he
comes
in
mist
but
who?

today
too
mist
life
in
a
little
house

with
umbrella-hats
farewell!
farewell!
thin
mist


farewell!
farewell!
hands
waving
lost
in
mist


my
house
where
even
mist
is
sloppy


misty
day
empty
silent
temple
hall


a
bell
clangs
life
slipping
by
evening
mist


me
and
Buddha
heads
lost
in
mist

world
over
Hell
viewing
spring
blossoms

plum-trees
blooming
even
Hell's
cauldrons
CLOSED

plum-trees
blooming
even
Hell's
gate
CLOSED

spring
peace
a
mouse
licking
Sumida
River

at
dawn
homeless
too
cat
crying
for
love

hey
big
cat
shake
a
leg!
the
wife
calls

smeared
with
garden
blossoms
the
lover
cat

staring
staring
in
a
mirror
lover
cat


a
grain
of
rice
stuck
to
his
nose
lover
cat

fool
cat
tied
up
still
crying
for
love


darkness
to
darkness
the
lover
cat

dirty
yes
but
the
cat
has
a
wife

spring
breeze
clutching
a
chopstick
sleeping
child

his
butt
blown
by
the
spring
breeze
roof-thatcher


spring
breeze
a
mouse
licking
Sumida
River

spring
breeze
grain
of
rice
in
the
stone
saint's
mouth


even
in
falling
snow
a
spring
breeze
blows

vespers
tears
shine
in
a
frog's
eyes
too

*Issa: Cup-of-Tea Poems*

blossoms
scattering
gaping
mouthed
waiting
frog

looking
me
over
with
a
grimace
frog

brazenly
squatting
on
the
straw
mat
frog

he
escapes
trickling
pee
croaking
frog

crossing
a
bridge
behind
a
blind
man
frog

scowling
up
at
the
evening
sky
frog

serene
and
still
mountain
viewing
frog

in
a
saint's
stone
hand
squatting
safe
frog

taking
a
leak
frog
keeps
on
croaking

praising
Buddha
mouths
gaping
wide
frogs

scrawny
frog
fight
on!
Issa
to
the
rescue

locked
in
a
staring
contest
with
a
frog

in
the
high
seat
boss
of
croaking
frogs

in
Buddha's
stone
hand
squatting
safe
frog

stone
still
for
the
smelling
horse
a
frog

from
the
great
bronze
Buddha's
nose
a
swallow

licking
a
bamboo
leaf's
spring
rain
mouse

morning
market
bare
chested
in
spring
rain

morning's
first
thing
hands
pray
in
spring
rain

pigeons
mating
crows
mating
spring
rain


the
nightingale's
rain
drenched
morning
voice

even
crapping
the
nightingale
sings
a
prayer


wafting
through
trees
beggar's
flute
and
nightingale

nightingale
warbling
the
east
gate
to
Heaven

nightingale
splish
splash
takes
a
rain
bath
singing

holy
water
font
nightingale
splashes
too


nightingale
for
the
emperor
too
same
song

gate
after
gate
making
the
rounds
butterfly


flitting
butterfly
to
Buddha's
lap
returns

bliss
to
be
reborn
a
meadow
butterfly

butterfly
dance
arrow
in
a
dying
deer

amid
butterflies
little
butterflies
mountain
home


stuck
to
the
dog
curled
asleep
butterfly

a
butterfly
stuck
fast
to
Buddha's
cheek


trusting
my
muddy
foot
a
butterfly
sleeps

sticky
sticky
dead
tree
blooming
butterflies

walking
across
the
hanging
bridge
butterfly

this
way
to
Zenkō
Temple!
butterfly
flies

borrowing
an
antler
the
butterfly
rests

counting
heads
in
a
hot-tub
butterfly

festival
day
white
monks
white
butterflies

sleeping
in
a
row
butterfly
cat
priest

Buddha's
saints
don't
care
cherry-trees
bloom

all
night
under
cherry
blossoms
bitching


Buddha's
saints
and
saviors
look
cherry
blossoms

great
Edo
in
every
nook's
nook
cherry
blossoms


lord
of
mountain
cherry
blossoms
stone
Buddha

even
Emma
Hell's
king
gawks
cherry
blossoms

*Issa: Cup-of-Tea Poems*

from
Japan's
front
door
on
cherry
blossoms

the
big
horse
rubs
his
butt
cherry
blossoms

wearing
umbrella-hats
into
blossoms . . .
clouds

a
lord
forced
to
dismount
cherry
blossoms

blown
to
the
wide
river
cherry
blossoms
light

most
end
up
stuck
in
mud
cherry
blossoms

splish
splash
sparrow
takes
a
blossom
bath


simply
trusting
cherry
blossoms
trickle
down


fluttering
down
garden
mulch
cherry
blossoms

blossoms
pile
blizzard
in
the
dog's
bowl


parasols
sticky
sticky
cherry
blossoms


to
the
west
cherry
blossoms
scatter
temple

the
big
cat
buries
a
piss
blossoms
snow

on
his
finger
one
penny
Buddha's
birthday


Buddha
even
in
the
beggar-town
is
born

horseflies
and
bees'
lucky
day
blossom
temple


the
ants'
road
leads
to
the
blossom
temple

Buddha
is
born
in
a
tossed
coin
shower

Buddha
in
the
midst
of
coins
is
born

little
cuckoo
sing!
sing!
Issa
is
here

lucky
lucky
most
lucky
day
'cuckoo'

crawling
across
a
bridge
far
below
'cuckoo'

great
Edo
from
nook
to
nook
'cuckoo'

stepping
in
an
Edo
garden
'cuckoo'

sing
soft
next
door
a
samurai
lives
cuckoo


singing
mountain
cuckoo
don't
fall
off
that
horse!


like
warbling
pure
haiku
mountain
cuckoo


mountain
cuckoo
sings
mister
toad's
funeral


temple
bell
and
mountain
cuckoo
taking
turns


does
the
caged
nightingale
hear?
mountain
cuckoo

now
the
skin's
peeled
off
snake
are
you
cool?

on
Buddha's
lap
a
snake's
forsaken
skin


just
as
he
is
becoming
Buddha
snail

tea-water
left
out
over
night
a
snail


at
my
feet
when
did
you
get
here?
snail

morning
rain
now
next
to
me
a
snail

home
village
on
Buddha's
face
a
snail

in
moonlight
going
bare
chested
snail


all
in
a
row
little
bean-sized
snails

the
brushwood
gate's
substitute
lock
a
snail


little
snail
no
different
asleep
awake

little
snail
inch
by
inch
climb
Mount
Fuji

joining
the
farmer's
afternoon
nap
a
snail

in
fifth-month
rain
squish
squash
strutting
crow

hidden
in
trees
praising
Buddha
rice-planter

beside
the
hotspring's
steam
they're
planting
rice

like
he's
snapping
at
the
downpour
gargoyle

watching
the
downpour
under
a
temple
bell

one
house
in
one
downpour
dead
center

darting
to
the
downpour's
beat
a
swallow

summer
downpour
naked
on
a
naked
horse

in
summer
cool
ambling
down
my
road
to
Hell

cool
like
hand-balls
peaks
of
clouds

it's
a
down
down
down-trodden
land
but
cool

spread-eagle
lying
in
bed
cool
lonely

in
summer
cool
account
book
for
a
pillow

summer
cool
the
gate
to
Buddha's
land

in
soup
kettle
in
toilet
summer
moon

mid-stream
taking
a
leak
summer
moon

a
beggar
child
plucks
and
sings
summer
moon

glimmering
morning-
glories
bloom
pure
water

in
a
poison
plant's
shade
pure
water


left
of
my
hut
pure
water
right
the
moon

mountain's
pure
water
people
muck
it
up


my
house
where
the
town's
fireflies
hide
out

they
have
kids
too
bridge
beggars
calling
fireflies

fly
away
fireflies
my
hut's
smoky!
smoky!


the
dog
sparkling
with
fireflies
sound
asleep


to
my
gate
they
come
on
purpose
fireflies


a
mouth
calling
fireflies
one
flies
in


tripping
in
the
old
hand's
wrinkles
firefly


do
you
think
my
hair's
a
thicket
firefly?

ちら〳〵と降る小数の羽せん

through
the
big
house
like
a
pro
firefly


blown
away
by
the
horse's
fart
firefly


house
in
deep
shade
high
noon
fireflies


first
firefly
smack!
into
people's
heads


my
home
where
I
even
exhale
mosquitos


one
more
wing-buzzing
mosquito
in
my
ear

naughty
child
tied
to
a
tree
calling
fireflies

if
we
quarrel
go
outside
first
firefly


on
my
sleeve
taking
five
done-in
firefly

down
in
the
soup
kettle
fireflies
fall


secluded
house
the
fireflies'
playground

at
my
pillow
at
my
feet
fireflies

biting
the
stone
Buddha
thicket
mosquito

Edo's
mosquitos
mean
and
big-city
bold!

driven
from
next
door
come
on
in
mosquitos

the
stone
saint
dead
center
in
blooming
pinks

in
a
saké-bowl
a
flea
swimming
swimming

a
flea
jumps
in
the
laughing
Buddha's
mouth

night
in
a
big
saké-bowl
the
moon
a
flea

dawn
to
Fuji!
to
Fuji!
fleas
jumping
off


tired
of
walking
a
wrinkled
arm
the
flea
jumps

the
mouth
that
gnawed
a
flea
praising
Buddha


bloated
flea
walking
it
off
up
a
tree

spare-time
work
picking
off
a
child's
fleas

counting
flea
bites
she
suckles
her
child

if
you
jump
flea
jump
on
the
lotus

mother
cat
gnawing
her
kitten's
fleas

knowing
the
priest
is
blind
brazen
straw-mat
fleas

new
straw
mat
fleas
jumping
bumpity
bump!

evening
hut
fleas
jumping
bumpity
bump!

our
world
even
walking
on
sand
fleas

strolling
up
the
mountain
out
back
temple
flea

chasing
behind
the
man
with
a
bow
fawn

oblivious
to
the
hunter's
arrows
fawn

the
ants'
road
from
peaks
of
clouds
to
here

the
rice-field
worker's
sunshade
peaks
of
clouds

burning
trash
in
a
garden
peaks
of
clouds


a
butterburr
leaf
pops
open
the
heat


Shinano
road
mountains
bearing
down
heat


a
hot
day's
treasure
little
clump
of
trees


hot
day
cool
abacus
for
a
pillow


spears
of
rice
are
grateful
summer
heat

a
rice-
growing
land's
lucky
lucky
heat

account
book
for
a
pillow
summer
heat

white
mountain
snow's
far-off
twinkle
the
heat

scowling
at
the
hot
summer
day
gargoyle

hot
night
bats
dangle
by
the
river

your
rice-field
my
rice-field
the
same
green

*Selected Haiku of Kobayashi Issa*

rice-fields
greening
greening
bamboo
flutes
play

swatting
a
fly
looking
at
a
mountain

I'm
going
out
enjoy
your
sex
hut's
flies

swatting
a
fly
and
praising
Buddha

swatting
a
fly
on
Buddha's
holy
head

if
I
go
out
they
go
out
hut's
flies

lacquered
tray
whoops!
the
fly
slips

one
man
one
fly
the
great
temple
hall

old
hand
swats
a
fly
already
gone

gaping
mouthed
fly-
hungry
dog
at
the
gate

temple
fly
mimic
hands
praying
beads

don't
swat
the
fly!
wringing
hands
wringing
feet

swat!
swat!
the
fly's
escaping
laughing
voice

a
spot
on
the
letter
that
swatted
a
fly


the
lacquered
tray
becomes
the
flies'
outhouse

like
it's
floating
on
lotus
leaves
hut


in
this
world
bristling
with
thorns
lotuses

our
world
where
rice-field
muck
grows
lotuses

this
world's
blooming
lotuses
are
bent

lotuses
too
slightly
bent
floating
world

blooming
lotuses
where
sewer
water
drains

raindrops
drip
drip
drip
first
autumn
dawn

autumn
dawn
just
saying
it
feel
lonely

do
you
know
it's
autumn's
dawn
butterfly?

autumn's
begun
unknowing
puppy
Buddha

autumn's
begun
unknowing
child
Buddha


autumn
dawn
a
cold
and
flu
raining
sky

autumn
dawn
just
saying
it
feel
old


morning-
glories
lush
on
a
house
elsewhere

in
morning-
glories
bare
shouldered
holy
man

deep
in
morning-
glories
children
hiding
out


morning-
glories
on
the
saw
scrap
heap
bloom


blowing
her
nose
in
morning-
glories
woman


born
again
morning-
glories
thrive
autumn


my
hut
is
a
morning-
glory
miser


thatched
with
morning-
glories
little
hut

peeking
out
of
morning-
glories
a
mouse

cool
morning-
glories
eating
my
rice
alone


trampling
my
sweet
rice-cake
singing
grasshopper

do
you
think
my
head's
grass
grasshopper?


gambling
in
the
grass
in
the
pot
grasshopper

moving
to
live
in
the
rice-box
grasshopper

don't
crush
the
beads
of
white
dew
grasshopper

crawling
out
the
wild
dog's
hole
grasshopper

grasshopper
in
scarecrow's
stuffed
gut
singing

grasshopper
even
as
they
sell
him
singing

to
the
grinding
teeth
beat
grasshopper
sings

atop
the
scripture
reader's
head
grasshopper

grasshopper
noon
and
night
just
bitching

I'm
taking
a
leak
look
out!
grasshopper


cheeks
stuffed
with
a
red
flower
grasshopper
sings

the
other
day
we
said
goodbye
dewy
grave


in
beads
of
dew
one
by
one
my
home
village

in
the
white
dew
vanishing
my
house

a
treasure
at
my
gate
pearls
of
dew

into
the
white
dew
splashing
struts
a
crow

taking
a
leak
adding
to
the
dewy
field

a
dewdrop
fades
done
with
this
rotten
world

the
old
wall's
grass
trusting
beads
of
dew

in
morning-
glories
how
many
cups
of
dew?

_Selected Haiku of Kobayashi Issa_

simply
trust!
trust!
dewdrops
spilling
down

my
hut
where
even
beads
of
dew
are
bent

looking
for
the
bead
of
dew
she
pinched
child

this
world
is
a
dewdrop
world
yes
but

lotus
leaf
dewdrops
plenty
for
morning
tea

lotus
leaves
in
this
world
warp
the
dew

leaf
to
leaf
tumbling
down
autumn
dew

in
vain
grass
dewdrops
forming
in
vain

on
the
Buddha
smoking
incense
morning
dew

the
youngest
child
visiting
graves
brings
the
broom

the
old
dog
leads
the
way
visiting
graves

wrinkled
face
he's
my
age
lanterns
for
the
dead

burning
for
someone
else
we
think
grave
lanterns

cold
grass
soaking
wet
lanterns
for
the
dead


an
orphan
led
by
hand
lantern
for
the
grave

by
votive
lantern
light
eating
rice
naked


one
dies
out
two
die
out
lanterns
for
the
dead

in
the
soup
kettle
stars
Heaven's
River

*Issa: Cup-of-Tea Poems*

flowing
in
the
hut's
gate
Heaven's
River

my
stars
are
old
men
too
Heaven's
River


in
cold
water
slurping
down
Heaven's
River

in
my
saké
down
the
hatch!
Heaven's
River


granny
drinks
her
saké
moonlit
night

wanting
to
grab
that
moon
crying
child

harvest
moon
going
out
going
back
in

mountain
village
in
soup
too
a
harvest
moon

hole
in
the
wall
come
on
in
harvest
moon

harvest
moon
on
the
mountain
scarecrow's
sleeve

turtle
and
moon
merge
Sumida
River

watch
my
key
pine-tree!
going
moon-gazing

harvest
moon-
gazing
priests
samurai
merchants

if
only
the
nag
were
here
harvest
moon


praise
Buddha
praise
Buddha
a
long
night

fleas
is
your
night
also
long?
lonely?


drawing
words
on
my
belly
a
long
night

autumn
wind
a
beggar
eyes
me
comparing

autumn
wind
ambling
down
my
road
to
Hell

in
autumn
wind
trusting
Buddha
butterfly

in
autumn
wind
this
year's
crop
red
leaves

a
few
teeth
left
whistling
autumn
wind

in
autumn
wind
gone
belly-up
grasshopper

the
calf
begins
his
journey
autumn
wind

in
autumn
wind
walking
away
firefly

in
autumn
wind
clutching
my
sleeve
butterfly

autumn
wind
red
flowers
she
wanted
to
pick

autumn
wind
winding
enters
my
gate

in
autumn
wind
a
homeless
crow
is
blown

onlookers
at
a
funeral
autumn
wind

eating
my
rice
in
loneliness
autumn
wind

off
in
a
corner
last
year's
prize-winning
mum

evening
wiping
horse-shit
off
my
hand
with
a
mum

prize-winning
mum
tears
in
an
old
man's
eyes

if
it
weren't
for
us
you'd
all
grow
crooked
mums

used
to
losing
I
don't
mind
mum-contest

losing
the
contest
surprise!
the
lord's
mum
won

the
great
lord
has
pull
chrysanthemum
contest

what
a
bitch
even
flower
blue-bloods
win

smelling
of
saké
smelling
of
piss
chrysanthemum

the
losing
mum
punished
in
a
corner

like
me
getting
lots
of
sleep
chrysanthemum

on
the
great
mum's
peak
asleep
caterpillar


morning
mist
is
tangled
in
the
willow


mountain
mist
moves
through
the
temple
hall


on
one
thicket
custom-made
evening
mist
hangs


daybreak
Asama's
mist
on
the
table
crawls


from
out
the
hanging
temple
bell
mist

mountain
mist
in
the
gargoyle's
gaping
mouth

cows
moo
moo
moo
out
of
mist
emerge

from
the
great
bronze
Buddha's
nostrils
mist

Iso
Temple
hall
fainter
and
fainter
mist

night
mist
horse
remembering
holes
in
the
bridge

mountain
temple
in
Buddha's
lap
mist

from
the
wild
dog's
howling
rising
mist

from
mountain
temple
gables
rising
mist

my
home
morning
mist
noon
mist
evening
mist

nightingale
crunch
crunch
struts
in
red
leaves

staring
at
the
man
burning
red
leaves
Buddha

a
young
buck
pissing
sticky
red
leaves

mother
watches
pony
leave
autumn
rain

cut
grass
sticking
to
boots
autumn
rain

mountain
garden
pigeons
cooing
autumn
rain

autumn
rain
the
weaned
pony
goes
to
market

snail
how
do
you
make
your
living?
autumn
rain

the
horse
drinks
medicine
too
autumn
rain

the
calf
begins
his
journey
autumn
rain

like
pebbles
pounding
the
eaves
autumn
rain


in
a
flash
the
lake
brimming
over
fireworks

in
a
flash
our
darkness
lighted
fireworks


Muen
Temple
bell
clangs
in
the
great
fireworks

putting
down
the
lord's
fireworks
Edo
mouths

arm
for
a
pillow
fireworks
ka-boom!
boom!

boom!
boom!
ka-boom!
all
are
duds
fireworks


even
one-
penny
fireworks
ooo!
ahh!

on
the
tip
of
Buddha's
nose
stinkbug


the
little
crow
is
scorned
rice-field
geese

geese
at
my
gate
cry
all
you
like
no
rice

*Selected Haiku of Kobayashi Issa*

wild
goose
neck
stretching
peeks
in
my
gate

autumn's
first
geese
crapping
on
people
fly
on

don't
cry
geese
everywhere
the
same
floating
world

begging
at
my
gate
the
geese
lose
weight

one
and
all
faces
of
Buddhas
cold
tonight

monkey
rides
mother's
back
in
night
cold

[77]

有川や篝声宅り〳〵遊々夕入

dawn's
cold
sneaks
through
a
hole
in
the
wall

an
old
man's
clogs
clack
clack
winter
moon

a
cold
moon
facing
the
cold
mountain
temple

like
he's
biting
at
the
cold
moon
gargoyle

cold
moon
wild
geese
praying
to
the
sea-god

a
snail
moves
in
with
me
first
winter
rain

feet
groping
for
the
stone
bridge
night
cold

my
hut
back
door
to
front
door
night
cold

wrinkles
from
top
to
bottom
night
cold

the
stomped-
at
mouse
escaping
laughing
night
cold

my
palms
stained
indigo-
blue
night
cold

the
young
folks
sleep
together
night
cold

first
winter
rain
the
world
drowns
in
haiku

in
winter
rain
bitter
faced
Buddhas

for
our
sake
sitting
in
winter
rain
Buddha

in
one
house
horses
people
winter
rain

the
door
latch
rusting
scarlet
winter
rain

crossroads
of
six
ways
I
stand
in
dead
grass

out
the
back
door
taking
a
wild
leak
first
ice

my
house's
only
face
towel
frozen
stiff

from
the
tip
of
Buddha's
nose
icicle

that's
using
his
head
priest
breaking
icicles

my
house's
first
icicle
gray
with
soot

all
kinds
of
fools
moon-gazing
winter
prayers

winter
prayers
a
cut-purse
too
in
moonlight

he
lets
me
cross
his
garden
winter
prayers


straight
through
rice-fields
going
to
winter
prayers

Buddha's
world
even
a
dog
at
winter
prayers


the
hut's
dog
escorts
going
to
winter
prayers

first
snowfall
worms
in
the
belly
sing

first
snow
first
dog-tracks
two-
penny
bridge

the
big
dog's
crap
paved
over
first
snow

first
snow
there's
someone
in
the
outhouse

the
first
snow
doesn't
quite
hide
it
dog-crap

mountain
temple
deep
under
snow
a
bell

falling
snow
in
straw
sandals
leaving
the
inn

to
my
open
palms
flitting
down
snow

deep
snow
and
right
above
Heaven's
River

my
village
bell
rings
deep
under
snow

it's
a
load
on
the
cow's
head
snow-pile

what
a
straight
pee-hole!
snow
at
the
gate

thin
snow
rolled
into
Buddha
by
a
child

a
sparrow
chirping
in
his
lap
snow-Buddha

growing
old
at
my
gate
snow-Buddha


even
our
fleeting
snow
becomes
Buddha

at
my
gate
the
snow-Buddha
too
scowls


palms
in
the
cooking
smoke
winter
cold

Shinano
road
mountains
bearing
down
cold

in
a
thatched
hut
even
dreaming
the
cold


wolf-shit
in
the
grass
how
cold
it
is


even
to
my
biased
eyes
my
shadow
cold


drawing
words
in
an
old
tray's
ashes
cold


even
to
my
biased
eyes
my
head
looks
cold


old
banner
in
a
thicket
flapping
cold

かくれ家や犬の鼻さきの燵かな

what
a
ruckus
kids
and
beach
plovers
mingle

the
reed
roof
white
with
sleeping
plover
crap

beach
plovers'
rising
ruckus
chased
by
a
dog

secluded
house
sweeping
soot
off
the
dog

by
a
pond
sweeping
soot
off
the
turtle

with
a
fan
I
sweep
my
sooty
house

down
to
the
bone
cold
a
little
lantern

through
a
thin
wall's
mouse-hole
enters
the
cold


a
luxury
for
Issa
one
bag
of
coal

great
lord
drenching
wet
passes
my
cozy
fire


here
and
there
in
little
meetings
plovers

what
a
huge
convention!
plovers
on
the
beach

from
the
great
bronze
Buddha's
nose
soot-sweeping

kindly
the
wind
sweeps
out
my
sooty
hut


cold
wind
a
24-cent
prostitute
shack

cold
wind
wrapping
sardines
in
oak
leaves


cold
wind
a
snoring
crescendo
trashy
house

kindly
cold
wind
sweeps
out
my
gate

*Issa: Cup-of-Tea Poems*

for
me
and
the
pine-tree
the
wretched
year
ends

come
what
may
trusting
Buddha
my
year
ends

clang!
bang!
the
wretched
year's
final
bells

a
wind-chime's
empty
babble
ends
the
year

downwind
from
the
horse's
fart
year's
end

a
child
Buddha
pointing
the
year
ends